Those Changing Roads

Poems
Shirley M. C. Johnson

ISBN: 978-1-963453-06-5

Book Design and Editing: John Jarvis

Illustrations:

Front Cover Art: Doan Trang L.--https://www.fiverr.com/doantrang/illustrate-anything-for-you-in-this-style

Back Cover Art: Milda Daniliauskaitė--https://unsplash.com/@mdaniliauskaite59?utmcontent=creditCopyText&utm_medium=referral&utm_source=unsplash

Family Section Photo, p.9: Image by Hans: https://pixabay.com/photos/apple-trees-apple-tree-plantation-5019016/

Friends Section Photo, p. 34: Image by Thomas G.: https://pixabay.com/photos/tree-deciduous-tree-landscape-fall-8411271

Photos pp. 1, 47, and 57: By Su Bailey, mosaic artist, photographer and stepdaughter of the author

First Edition 2025

Park Edge Creative, LLC
48 Park Edge Avenue
Springfield, MA
www.parkedgecreative.com

DEDICATION

I would like to dedicate this book to Dr. John Jarvis, who has been a consistent cheerleader to me over the last several decades (with his own version of appropriate black cheerleading attire), and also someone who offered to become my editor. He has fulfilled that function with grace and unremitting patience and humor. That offer and his work represent a level of friendship that expands the definition of that term. Thank you, John.

TABLE OF CONTENTS

WELCOME TO MY WORLD

A friend of mine recently said: "It's a surprise each morning to wake up alive." Of course I had to agree with that. As the years accumulate, we see things differently because there is so much history behind us, and because the parameters of our lives keep changing. We lose family members and old friends, even new friends, and with them the joys of those relationships, even though they leave us with important memories to embrace.

Fortunately, there are also parts of our daily lives that remain stable and meaningful. For my sister-in-law Audrey, it was baking. Even though she had lupus, when she said she had baked something that day, I knew it was a good day. For me, it's people I know and have known, the art in my life, gardening, nature in general, and trees. This is why I chose photographs of trees to illustrate this little book. Trees keep the planet alive–and make me grateful that I'm still alive.

--Shirley

Little Therapy Poems

Other people may have therapy dogs
In their lives,
But I have therapy poems.
They are there waiting for me
To unleash them,
Waiting around the corner on my laptop,
Ready to help me deal with whatever is vexing,
Or assailing me,
Or helping me figure out how to handle the aging
That can deliver a new surprise for me
Almost every day.

These poems have helped me process
Whatever is going on in my life:
The recent deaths in my family,
My brother and then my sister-in-law
In particular,
Because their passing meant something
That other deaths haven't.
Without parents and siblings
I feel like an orphan
Stranded in the middle of an island
Of memories no one else can affirm
Or share.
Now I've begun to understand
What others have talked about and felt
About this same kind of loss.

And then there's the joy in remembering
All the friends
Who have left their marks on me.
Brilliant tattoos on a soul
That you can wear anywhere,
Even at holiday get-togethers

Without covering them up.

These poems have given me a way
To adapt to whatever might come next,
And to remember what came last.
Perhaps they can trigger your own
Special memories,
As I share mine.
Or so my other friends,
The ones who don't require hard drives
Or live in the clouds,
Have convinced me could happen.
We will have to see
If they are right.

FAMILY:

The Journeys We've Made Together

A Love Affair

She saw him often in church, sitting across the room
And then, later, at the local ballroom,
With his wavy hair and stunning blue eyes, she said,
Always searching her out.
They went home together that night
And many nights after that.
Together for seventy-two years
Until he left her on another trip.

They built a small house and a family of four together,
Living frugally
Making do with his welding skills that made use of what others
no longer kept,
Turning it into good stuff, just not new,
Her canning and freezing, always working hard,
And side by side.
Planning and then going on fishing and camping trips:
The best entertainment for a thrifty family.

A good man, but also hard,
Wanting his way, because he felt he earned it,
And that's the way it should be,
And she, the sweet wife and mother,
Knowing how to make it all work
At his side, still smiling, and cooking her own good stuff.

Now she is on her own,
Maybe enjoying her last days,

Making her own decisions,
Playing bingo when she wants to,
Eating with friends when she wants to,
Staying up late when she wants to,
And calmly getting ready to go
On her own last trip.

(Written after my brother died on October 12, 2023.)

A Long Journey Home

"God must be really busy now.
There's a lot going on,"
She said.
"He just doesn't have time to prepare a place for me,
But I will be ready when He is."
So she played bingo,
And laughed when she won a little carton of animal crackers,
Or $1.40 at dime bingo.
Always happy to talk on the phone,
Whenever I called.
She continued to take her walker to the dining room,
Or to hear a musician,
Until, as time progressed,
 She couldn't anymore.
And then she waited
Calmly
With her children by her side
To go home at last.
Now we are left
With our own now painful, and sweet, memories
Of someone like no other.
The cherry pie she made for me
When I visited from wherever I was living at the time.
No one could make it better
With fruit she and my brother picked themselves.
Or even earlier,
Remembering all the Sunday dinners
She served my mother after church
Those years my mother lived alone.
Always kind

Always there for her.
And when my mother was gone
For me.
She was a Christian
Like no other.
No wonder God found the time to finally bring her home.

(A tribute to my sister-in-law, Delores, written on August 31, 2024,
two days after she died in hospice care and a month before her 92nd
birthday.)

Potato Talk

The groundhogs enjoyed my new organic yellow potatoes
So much
They didn't leave very many for me to try.
And my brother was no longer around
To help me mourn my loss.
Now I just am left to mourn both my potatoes
And him.
Alone.
For no matter what was going on in my life
I always had potatoes
To talk about
In my weekly phone calls.
Raised on a farm
With a gardening mother,
We learned to love new potatoes,
Especially with cucumber salad,
Fresh picked from the garden.
She taught us how to "steal" the new potatoes,
To keep the babies growing.
No matter what was going on
In his life or mine,
A stroke for him,
A bad back for me,
Potatoes kept us
Connected.
And stole away

Our differences.

How can you not feel abiding affection

For someone who shares

Your love of buttery new potatoes?

(Written after the death of Delores. Her death made me realize the depth of pain to lose both of them. Now both of them were gone, with neither of them to answer the weekly phone calls I had made over the years to her and to my brother Bud. He had died less than a year before her on October 12, 2023.)

Dirt

Everywhere there was dirt
My mother fought it
In the corners, on the carpets, in the stairwell,
And even on the stairs to the basement.
She filled her dustpan like the collection plate
My father passed around at church on Sundays.
On the farm with cows
No fear:
There was always a more than generous amount of dirt
Waiting for her inside.
But outside,
In her garden,
She could bask in the splendor
Of her now black soil,
Religiously enriched with abundant manure
Slowly marinated in straw bedding.
No need to fight unwanted dirt here.
It was all her rich and lovely loam meant for planting.
Dear Mother Nature, she'd murmur,
Just not for collection in my house.

Love Poem (For My Mother)

You

      have washed and cooked
      and most of all baked (because it made you feel creative)
      and slept with your husband for twenty-eight years;

      sat on the benches talking to the old ladies
      while your man danced and drank and told you to go home
      early if you wanted to;

      learned how to drive the Model T
      by getting into the car alone
      one afternoon;

      said you loved your husband
      because he was always a good provider.

You

      have become yourself again
      with other women;

      too old to change much
      but young again—it seems—
      with friends.

(Written in 1971 when she was 68)

A New Fan

How did they all live without air conditioning
Or even fans?
These hardy women, from pioneer stock,
Cooking and baking and even canning
In all that heat?

She was amazed,
Sitting in front of my most recent gift
Of a fan.
Why did my mother never think to buy one for herself,
I wondered?
It changed her life.
She seemed to be happier that summer,
Working in the kitchen
With her new fan by her side.

Memories of My Dad

I never really got to know my Dad
Because he died when I was nine,
But I knew how much I loved the things he did for me.

One day, I remember, he came home with his cap
Almost full of the raspberries he had picked for me
When he was out checking on the cows
Because he knew how much I loved them.
And when he returned from his many trips
To the Mayo Clinic
He always brought back something special for me.
The dresses were pretty,
But the pants appliqued with apples
Were my favorite
Because we had an apple orchard
And I got to pick up the apples on the ground
With him
For Mom's apple pies
And our appreciative hogs.

My older brothers
Who were eleven and sixteen years older than me,
Knew a different father,
One who was more demanding,
Sometimes a tough taskmaster,
They told me later.
But also always a hard worker,
Who didn't complain,
Even when he was sick
And dying of cancer.

When he died,
We all shared one precious memory together:
The box of chocolate-covered cherries
With a dollar bill scotch-taped to the top,
Waiting for us when we returned from church
On Christmas Eve,
His annual gift to each of us in the family.
For years afterwards
We talked about that ritual
And how much we missed it
And him.
As I still do, even all these years later
When I am the only one left from those days.
I just won't be eating that too-sweet candy
Anymore.

He Was a Renaissance Man

Our divorce cost $35;
That's $17.50 a piece,
Because he did all the paperwork,
And I supplied the information about the cause.
In Wisconsin at that time
You could only get a divorce for a (good) cause.
Mine was considered a very good one in those days:
I didn't want to have his (or anyone else's) children.
Of course, Dick knew that before we got married—
He just didn't want to believe me.
But we remained good friends,
Seeing each other often over the years.
In fact, my second husband and I even lived with him
For a while
When we moved to Seattle.

Dick was an amazing man.
He had earned two bachelor's degrees at the same time,
A master's degree,
And a Ph.D in something entirely different.
He loved chemistry and philosophy and history,
So why not earn degrees in them when he could,
He thought, and I agreed.

It still hurts me to think that someone so smart
And versatile
Would die so young.
Gone at sixty.

During our marriage
He had been a substitute high school teacher
Who could handle just about anything and anyone from
Woodworking class
To chemistry and physics and mathematics,
And German,
And even once or twice, special ed.,
Because he knew a lot
And could tell great stories
And develop amazing activities on the spot.
For a while he worked as an industrial chemical salesman
So that I could finish my degree,
And, once again, was loved by his employer
Because he could actually give good advice to his clients
When he answered their questions.
He obviously was very successful
At whatever he chose to do,
And made our lives as graduate students
More comfortable than they might have been.

After investing $35 in our new lives,
He continued to explore fields in and out of academia,
Successfully working in the California computer industry,
For a while,
Which accommodated his roving mind,
And lined his wallet for his new wife and stepchildren.

Through it all
He remained humble, a great storyteller,
And always an adventurous professional.
And, I was told,
A truly loving stepdad.

To Charles, the Dreamer

A horse walked slowly down the meadow, grazing
Contentedly.
Such are the ways we see the world, full of content
Or dissatisfaction,
  warmth
  happy colors
  or angry skies.

Everywhere the smell of fecund earth,
Decaying and growing things unknowingly,
We assess nature, give it shape,
And irony where once there was only
  change.

I see you, standing in the sun, smoking a cigarette,
Gazing off into the trees.

I see nothing. I don't know what it is you see.

Perhaps you are dreaming, as lovers, and old folks do,
Of special times and far-off places.

Perhaps you are just resting,
With only the earthworms moving slowly beneath you.

No matter
What you are, I can smile,
  and make you another.

You, your lovely Shires, and sheep, and geriatric chickens,
      crafting your dreams
      while I craft my own.

(Written sometime in the mid-1980's in rural Butler, Missouri, on the 80-acre farm my husband Charles and I chose together.)

A Pastoral Convention

It's the farm's fault
One damn day grabs the next one by the neck
And strangles it before I have a chance
To break them apart.

How can I start to make a change
When all around me animals are dying
And being born
In confused succession.

My world is full of shit,
All kinds and colors and shapes of it
Everywhere I walk, with friends and dogs,
Always someone steps in it.

We laugh of course,
We're very cosmopolitan
On our prairie farm
Set up from proceeds of years of urban living.

Really, daughter, says my mother,
You shouldn't watch that.
She's referring, I think, to all the breeding
Going on.
This time of lovely equine bodies, mounting,
Biting, spraying, winking,
And taking time, of course, undaunted,
To have a crap.

I grab her round the neck,

During one of those rare moments,
And hug her, laughing
At my life.
We break apart, still smiling,
And misunderstood.

(My oldest brother and sister-in-law drove Mom to our farm in Missouri in 1984
to see where we lived. No surprises for me about Mom's reaction. After all, she
had spent most of her life on a farm, knowing how hard the work always had been.)

Trees Are Family Too

I always look forward to looking out my window,
No matter where I live,
Because usually there will be a tree
Or even a lot of trees
To look at—and admire.
When I bought my condo,
I had a peaceful view of wooded wetlands
Which I relished every day.
And when I had visited my new companion
For the first time,
With amazement
I looked out at the same view.
In retrospect,
I don't know
Whether my love
Came to be just for him
Or maybe because of all his trees.
(As he would say: That's a joke.)

However, whenever I look at trees
I feel a kinship
Because I have many of the same feelings
With them
As I do with people.
I feel comforted by being surrounded by them
In the woods or in my yard.
I feel sorrow
When they are sick or slowly dying.
Happy when they come back in spring
Complete with new leaves

To visit
Until they bear fruit in fall.
And even more exuberant when I see a bird's nest
Hidden away--
A surprising gift from the tree
For both the bird and me.

No wonder we are happier
When we can be silent in nature
Ready to hear only those special sounds
That make all other louder sounds disappear,
Even for a little while.
Like sitting in a room with someone
We care about
Without talking.
Just happy to be together.

My Traveler Man

I saw him for the first time
Standing next to a desert plum van
In a parking lot at a restaurant
Where we'd agreed to meet.
The huge van was a clue that he'd been traveling
Or still was.
He was tall and lanky
Like my previous husband,
With big feet.
Match.com had come up with a good candidate.

We left the restaurant to visit a local art museum,
Another good sign.
We connected in all sorts of good ways,
And our relationship began
And then blossomed.

We went traveling together in a trailer we bought together,
Across the country twice,
Then on cruise ships to the South Pacific, the Amazon, the Baltics,
and Iceland,
Stayed in apartments in Leiden, Venice, Rome, and Nafplio.
He took longer trips
To sail around the world on his own,
And see places he'd read about as a kid:
The Great Wall of China, Japan, Indonesia, the Antarctic, Greenland,
And all the ports along the way
On those three long trips
I couldn't do with a bad back
And less interest in being on a ship

For ninety days in a row.
He was a sailor
And loved boats,
Having built one way back when,
And purchased nine or was it ten sailboats
Over the years.

I'm a gardener;
He's a sailor;
We're the mud couple,
Who now are aging out of it all.
Twenty-two years later
We sit across from each other
Talking about those past trips,
All the great memories of so many things and places:
Puffins on the Shetland Islands,
The Hermitage, the Manaus Opera House,
Whatever comes to mind for us.
And all the creatures, people, and scenes
He alone has seen,
As he keeps wondering
If there might be one more trip
We could make/ he could make,
Because thinking that his traveling days
Are over
Is almost too much to bear.

Growing old isn't fair, we say.
Our parents never warned us what it would be like,
To have to give up so much of what we loved to do and see
And be.

It's like a child learning to walk:
We're having to craft a new way to move through the world,
Falling down
And getting up again,
Holding on to objects and ideas
To keep moving forward
Toward that second cup of coffee,
And now,
Small electric boat.

They Come in All Sizes

I never wanted to have children.
When I was twelve, I remember thinking
That taking care of children
Wasn't all that much fun,
Even when I got paid for it.
And the poor mothers I worked for
Seemed to be thinking about their children
All the time.
I couldn't figure out
When they had time to read a book.
That seemed like a really unhealthy situation
To be in.
And, quite frankly,
I never changed my mind
About that.

Now, over seventy years later,
I'm a stepmother.
The two kids in their 50s and 60s
Seem like the perfect age for children.
They can take care of themselves.
When they show up, they do projects,
Willingly work just for food,
And leave even before you want them to.

Although they eat a lot more
Because they are a lot bigger than any young child,
Even a whole lot bigger for a time,
And might be allergic to one food group
Or another,
But they can actually cook,
And don't ask for money
For a new phone, gas, or college tuition,
Even though they might be given special gifts

Just because you haven't had to invest in them
In previous years.
All in all,
I would recommend being a stepmother,
If, like me, you never wanted to change diapers,
Or be on duty 24/7
For a job, or a life.

FRIENDS:

The Folks You Want Along for the Ride

Progression: To Louise

Sitting here in the sun
Next to you
Looking down at my body
And over at yours,
I wonder how we will make it
All those years later,
You and I,
Our bodies autographed in wrinkles
From old lovers
And new places
We have been.
Changing
Always changing,
A circular staircase
Winding up by slow paces
To the attic
With many windows.

(Written in the mid-1960's, early in our college years of sunbathing. We've remained friends, though, after I left Wisconsin, long distance ones with regular annual visits and other forms of communication.)

A Little Story: To Jeffrey

One day a gopher named Jeffrey
Came out of his hole.
"Oh, my," said Jeffrey, seeing bright green grass,
Smelling good as dreams
And sunshine shining.
"I think I will go off to see the world."
So he waved goodbye
To his Mom's potato salad
And set off never to return
(for a while).

Soon he saw a house tumble-downing,
"Aha," he thought, "I think I will stay here for a while."
So Jeffrey stayed
Making the gopher scene
Until one day
He remembered the smell of yellow sun and lovely roots.
He smiled to think of it.
He smiled so wide
He had to laugh and dance around.
He danced and danced, and danced some more.
Other gophers saw him and asked, "Do gophers dance?"
But Jeffrey just kept dancing . . .
yellow sun . . . green grass . . . roots . . . thick fur and, oh, thin fur.

"My my," they remarked to each other as he danced
Down the world shining.
"I wonder what's come over him."

(Jeffrey was a dear college friend without whom those college years in Madison
would not have been half as much fun for any of us. When he graduated, he left
to return to New York, married a dancer, and then drifted into finance and a
whole different kind of life from the one we'd led together in college.)

To Janet (No, now, J. Max) Growing Fat and Happy (Aren't You?)

I imagine you growing inches
Like vegetables in your backyard
Watering them every day
When you remember.
An inch to celebrate your divorce,
From a man
Who didn't have a clue
Who you were.
An inch for an old friend,
One of the few who still writes
When you do.
And there's one, maybe two
Or three or four
For your new woman love,
Who loves you in the morning,
When you look in the mirror
Together
Bleary-eyed and thick with sleep
Smiling at your new bulges
Like golden apples on an apple tree.
Ready for picking.

(Janet who became J. Max, walked out into the world in new clothes with a new name. She was a funny woman, one of my students, who remained a good friend. She became what she needed to be.)

Prosze Pani, Do Not Cry
(To My Polish Friend on Her Anniversary)

Prosze, Pani, do not cry.
You are not alone, dear lady,
With your new eyes crying
Over old love dying.
He still loves you
He still needs you
He just does not understand
What it feels like to drown in love
Over fried eggs and perfectly cooked bacon.
Tomorrow, maybe, with strong morning coffee
He will have a vision
Of growing old together
In the country
Flowers exploding with color behind you
And all will be as it used to be
When you were new lovers
Meeting in strange places
To exchange secret kisses
And drink imported wine.

(To a dear Polish friend whom I still email to stay in touch. She and her husband
live in the country most of the year now, and they do live among an explosion of
floral color, while her husband lives with cancer and has lost much of his own
color. *Prosze* is an often-used "please"; *Pani* is a form of address like our "Ms.".)

Obituaries

Someone I read recently
Said to write our own obituary
Every year.
I guess to put everything in our lives
Into perspective,
Or to give it meaning
When we're flailing
Around
Looking for it, that is,
Until we don't have to flail
Anymore.
Well, I guess mine would be:
I was born, went to college, worked, got married a few times,
Retired,
And now dying could be next,
I guess.
That pretty much sums it up.

And then I got an email from Legacy.com
To commemorate the death of a dear friend
Who had died eight years before.
What I had written on that site years earlier
Makes it clear
What's been important to me
About him:
His patience and good spirit as a teacher,
Kindness to his friends–and enduring devotion to his wife.
In my commemoration, I also mentioned my last trip to see him
And his wife, Joyce,
who was then in an Alzheimer's ward.

When we visited Joyce together,
To whom he fed lunch almost every day,
I saw what a challenge that was,
And admired him even more
For his sweet and loving care.
I also heard from one of the nurses
That he brought them a pie
Quite often as a thank you gift
For their own special care.
(And he was a really great baker.)
He also fed me that day,
The catfish he had caught just for me,
He said,
Before I showed up,
Setting off the smoke alarm,
While frying it really hot
The way he said it had to be done.
But now the smoke alarm
Was set to the music
Of our barely controlled laughter.
He hoped that that experience,
I think,
Would soften the blow
Of seeing my friend Joyce
In such a diminished state.

Dennie was many things,
Among that long list, also an inspired storyteller,
But for me
Most of all,
He was a loving and caring person
And a marvelous friend.

That's how I would like to be remembered
Too.

(Dennie was a colleague in the 80's from our Cottey College Missouri days who remained a friend until he died in 2016. We or I visited them as a couple, and then him wherever he lived, and he, us. Joyce had died two years earlier after many years in care.)

To Elsie, with Love

I have a friend who reads books
The way other people eat potato chips,
With devotion and commitment
To the process of finishing
The book (or bag of chips),
Or, in her case, the current pile of books.

And now her neighbors,
Her main source of all these (gently used) books,
Are moving away,
With their friendships and their ongoing commitments
To her entertainment
And her mental health.

But she will soldier on,
With others stepping in
As they always will
To provide her with the grit
For her stories about lives
She reads about
And the lives she's lived
These ninety-seven years.

Her own stories are always full of details
About her teaching—or much later, tutoring—of many students
In many places and of all ages.
English as a second language wherever she lived,
Struggling new college students in Massachusetts,
Children on the Sioux reservation in South Dakota,
Also as grant writer, teacher and principal,

In Texas and Oklahoma.
So many years of helping others,
Wanting to make a difference,
And never subtracting from their sense of self worth
In the process of her helping them along the way
To something better.

Now she's our stalwart supporter
Of whatever we are doing
Or plan to do.
A phone companion
For those of us fortunate to have our number
In her rapid dial.
She spends her days talking on the phone, surrounded by books
And newspapers, magazines, and flowers
That her daughter and son-in-law tend
For their pleasure and hers
And everyone who passes by.
A glorious natural world is one she celebrates
Every day
In every season.
A lesson for all of us to learn.

How does she remain not only ambulatory,
At ninety-seven,
But also so engaged in everything that is going on,
In her community, her country, and her life,
Often to consternation with it
And the people who are unkind to each other
Or self-serving.
That brings darkness to her discussions
And sometimes waning hope

For the future
When she no longer
Can make a difference,
In myriad small ways,
And others might not
Care enough to fix
What is wrong or broken.
But then looking at the trees
Outside her window
Always brings her back
To us
With a smile.

A Lifeline for Living

I can't imagine
What life would have been like
Without Beverly and Marlene
Who lived down the hill from me
On the farm
In grade school,
Before and after my father died.
Or Lorraine, Dianne, Bev, and Luanne
Who took the sting out of being different
In high school.
Like most women,
I can make my list of women friends
Who helped me weather
Whatever life threw at me,
Wherever I lived—
Some in person,
Others over the phone
Or internet
As I moved
To different places
And jobs.
Women who were more reliable
Than (many) men,
And even more fun
Than some.

We women need other women
Who don't always try to solve our problems
For us,
But listen with their eyes

As well as ears
And do it quietly
When not raucously.
Sharing recipes for excess zucchini,
Stories of excess hubris
Or fumbles
Out there in the firmament of politics
Or life in general
To make us laugh.

And now,
We also share our ever-lengthening lists of body parts
And systems
Gone or going
Awry.
That still can make us laugh
At our sagging parts
And cry
About each other's more difficult challenges
And changes
Together.

Observations Along the Way

Egg Women, Flower Women, Old Polish Women

I wonder what the old women would say to me
If I could understand them
The egg women, the flower women, the old Polish women
On the corners, in doorways, by the stores.
They don't smile much, these women
Grown old with their wicker baskets.

They are matter-of-fact:
Two *zlotys* an egg, some jonquils, a bunch of pine.
Only one woman smiles
A tired old servant smile,
Grown old from watching.
This old Polish woman
Whose eyes
Are like my grandmother's,
Kneading bread on Saturdays.
She knows something I don't know,
This old flower woman
With dirty hands and old wool cape.

(A *zloty* is a unit of Polish currency. Poles under Communism were allowed to
sell a limited number of things for cash when I was there in 1973-4 as a Fulbright
Visiting Professor. Out my apartment window I could see these women sitting on
stools selling a few types of things, including the three stems of flowers tied with
a ribbon that people would buy to take with them when they visited someone or
were invited for a meal. It provided a much-needed splash of color to the
greyness of most of the buildings.)

Sunday Carrion

They are sniffing over my past
Like giant nostrils
These women in their run-down heels,
Housedresses and Pendleton jackets.
They look for stains on sheets,
And bargains on old glassware,
Jewelry and dishes.
"Ah, what a lovely patterned little bowl."
(I won't smile at her
She will have to stroke the bowl alone.)

In the kitchen the phone rings;
It is a man responding to my rummage sale ad.
He got my number,
He said,
And wants to crawl all over my body.

I'm too tired from my ladies
To reply.

(Written in the late 70s after one of my many rummage sales, this time before
leaving Seattle.)

The Many Shades of Orange

I used to love orange.
I bought gorgeous orange rugs
And coverlets
And then bright curtains to match them
When I lived in Poland that year
With my second husband.
A trip to Cepalia, the folk art store,
Was a treasured destination,
Because there was always more folk art
To purchase with my American dollars
Made from teaching at a Polish university.

Years later, as a widow I met my current love
On match.com
By way of an orange cover on a book he wrote.
It seemed an omen of the lovely days past
Spent with bright orange and green and brown
In the background of my life.

It is 2024 and now the color
Has lost its luster for me.
It is ever-present in a current presence
Who has become associated with orange
By the color of his skin and hair.
Now, orange, a harbinger of chaos
And disruption.
Orange no longer relished for its brightness,
Now just darkness and foreboding
For what's to come.

Time to turn to people we love,
Others we can help along their way,
Enjoy the colors of nature
All the shades of green, brown, white,
And a gentler shade of orange.
Turn to the valiant artists who create, build, sculpt, paint, sing, dance
Their visions for the future.
Ones we can embrace
With pain or sorrow, but most of all, joy,
Whatever is needed to keep living
A life we can feel good about
No matter what.

A Poem to Dark Matter

The world is full of it.
Oh, dear.
From baby butts to clean,
To picking it up when walking the dog,
Shoveling it from one place to another,
Or using it—this time, wisely--to make compost
To grow our vegetables
And other good things to eat.

We are embarrassed by our own,
And other's excretions
But mumble endlessly and piteously
When our own internal system has gone awry
And witness nothing, or too much, to clear the dark matter away
For that particular day.

And then,
There are politicians who feed us
Rank and odoriferous statements
That would not even,
Or ever,
Oh, dear,
Make good compost.

Bananas

My first experience with bananas
Was as a babysitter.
The man of the house
Was home one day
And decided to fix his lunch before leaving for work.
All he could find to make was a peanut butter sandwich.
He toasted the bread.
(I guess it was stale.)
And then he added a banana,
Because, perhaps,
He couldn't find the new jar of jam.
I absolutely loved it;
I never forgot that taste
And seldom made that sandwich with jam
Again.

We didn't have bananas at our house;
We had apples from our orchard,
And boxes of peaches
During the summer
To can with saccharine for my Dad,
Because he had diabetes
And couldn't eat sweet stuff.

But as a grown up
I was introduced to all types of dishes
With bananas:
Banana splits; banana bread; banana flambe.
I really never knew much about them, though.
They were just in the stores—

And then
When I saw bananas
Hanging from the trees,
I felt really stupid
Because I had never known
That they grew facing upwards.

We take lots of things for granted.

A Different Perspective

Daylight Savings Time is coming soon,
So is spring.
I should have placed my order for organic potatoes
By now
As I have done every other year
For a lot of years.
But I haven't
Because I don't trust the past
To be a helpful guide
For the future.
Will it be such a wet spring
That my lovely seed potatoes
All rot
And so I should hold off planting them?
Or will it be another drought this year
That I can't keep up with the watering
From our solitary well?
How will Mother Nature penalize us
This year
For what we've done to her home?
We are the children
Who have misbehaved
Again and again,
And she appears to have lost patience
With us all.
And we cannot predict
How she will punish us
Now.

Or will the groundhogs return

(Or have they never left)
To feast on my little new potatoes
Before I get my share?

It appears that gardening
Has now become like religion:
We must have faith
That what we have believed in
Since we were little kids
Is still worth embracing
Even though again and again
We wonder why a God
Would do that to us,
Whatever the *that* is.
However,
Is there any real alternative to belief
If we are to have lovely new potatoes
On our table
One more time.

Perhaps I should just take to heart
What my funny, wry sixty-nine-year old nephew said to me
Yesterday:
"I'm just not going to worry
About my fatty liver
Anymore."

AGING

A Holiday for All Seasons

"Every day's a holiday when you know you're dying."
That was the greeting on my 1970's Christmas card
When I was still making them myself.
It shocked a few of my friends
(Not that I'd made my own cards:
I often did that).

Now it seems an especially apropos
Greeting for just about any occasion.
We're getting ready for the 4th of July,
Engulfed in wildfires, floods, our first hurricane of the season,
A Supreme Court in keeping with natural disasters,
Cyclones, devastation wherever you care to look
On the news or on social media.

Nice to think that every day can be a holiday
With fireworks, our favorite foods—
Or great junk food,
And friends or family gathered
To celebrate our imminent end,
Together.

Or not.

Reflections

I may have gotten all A's on my eighth grade report card,
But only a passing grade in high school physical education,
Wearing my royal blue bloomers.
Obviously, winning no contests in that attire,
Except for generating the most laughter of my friends.
Then there is my failing the contest
Of identifying which way faces East in our house,
And how to figure out how to get home from someplace else,
Or which way to get back on the trail—enroute to my car,
Or in the parking lot of the shopping center.
But I do know left and right,
Because my mother was able to teach me that early in our travels
In our '55 Chevy.
And then there's gardening:
Why do I have so much trouble growing tomatoes?
It's the one vegetable (I know it's a fruit, O.K.?)
That anyone really cares that much about.
So why is early--or maybe late--blight waiting for my plants
To provide fodder for them?
My peas, beans, cucumbers, potatoes, Swiss chard, and lettuce
Do just fine.
But who cares about them in this household
When only tomatoes matter.
Life goes on,
And I stumble from day to day
Trying to find my way back to sanity—and my car.

(Note: I found my report card in the old suitcase in which I keep memorabilia
that my mother saved from our various stages of life together and apart. That
was the only report card, so who knows what the others looked like. I know I
was a good student, but I don't know how good.)

The Joy of Being Alive

What a joy it is to be alive.
Despite all the hand-wringing
On TV
Over children being killed
By other children,
Or by adults
Who have bigger guns and missiles and rockets,
And get to kill more people at a time.
We still fret about the cost of meat
Or milk, or fruit,
And keep mowing our lawns on the weekends
As usual.

These lawns are spelling our future doom
In the circle of nature that we ignore.
But planting native plants
Occasionally,
If they are pretty
(Or not),
Could save us
And our food.

It is said by wise women
Of the past,
We do not inherit the earth,
From our ancestors:
We borrow it from our kids,
And the others who follow us
Who might have turned out
Smarter than us

If we had not doomed them
To floods, and fires, and hurricanes
With endless fury.
If we choose not to have Holsteins for our table
Now
With all the methane they emit
And land and water they use,
Maybe
We will have the joy of being alive
A while longer.

Nothing Much

Some days I'm real good
At nothing.
Things just won't fall into place
The way they should.
My new shoes don't feel quite right:
Did I get the wrong size, I wonder?
The car seems dirtier than usual
If that's possible.
And the electric can opener
Won't open the can of tuna for lunch.
The day is not off to a great start.

Of course, it could be worse.
I could have to run to the dentist again
The way I had to not so long ago
For a cracked tooth.
Or, to the doctor again for a tiny tick
That, who knows, could carry Lyme disease.
Or hear about someone I care about
Who has ended up in the hospital
With some awful disease or condition.
Or see that the groundhog is back
To drive me crazy
Just a while longer.
Since I'm good for nothing much today,
Guess I'll just have to give it up,
Instead of driving myself crazy.
Sit down with a nice cup of tea
Read a good book,
And hope the next day is better.
That's the hard-earned wisdom of old age.

Another Memoir

I'm thinking of how I'd use eternity,
Sitting at the controls of my memory
Stopping
Lengthening the time it took somethings to happen,
Moving backwards and forwards
Stopping
Looking
Choosing
The love times.
Smiling out a window
At branches, I think,
Of bittersweet,
For three quarters of eternity
If I wanted to.

(A poem from long ago, or perhaps from the future?)

Other Dirt

"So why aren't you smiling?" She asked by looking at me,
As she watched me digging a hole, removing all the rocks in the way.
I needed a really big hole for the tomato plant that was going there.
I get tired of all the rocks—we're in Stonington,
So I should be used to that by now.
But I'm not.
I grew up elsewhere.
I struggle to make every piece of ground
Stone-free.
Now I know why there are so many lovely stone fences
Everywhere you go in New England:
Centuries of back breaking digging
By men, women, and children,
Just to stay alive.
You've got it easy,
You dig for pleasure,
And stop when you want to.
You're a dog.
I want to be a dog.

(To my companion and dirt buddy, Dupcia, who spent many happy
hours hanging out and digging in the garden with me.)

Mother Nature

A friend told me I had to write a poem to groundhogs
Because I talk about them all the time.
So I did.
Because they invaded my garden,
Dug a huge hole in the front lawn,
One next to the house,
And another one in my psyche,
They are too smart for me.
No matter what I tried,
They still got the tomatoes
Before they ripened,
Eating half,
Though graciously, I guess,
 Leaving the other half
To ripen
For me.

My mother always said I had to share
My toys and candy or food
With the neighbor kids
Or my visiting cousins,
So I slowly learned how to deal with that,
Though I'd always grumble a little.
Now I try to accept the fact
That mother nature,
Like my mother,
Is teaching me to share
My food
With creatures of all sizes
No matter how many legs

And what language they speak
Or don't speak.
Because we are all on this earth
Together,
Trying to get by
Together,
Though grumbling
A little.

Philosophy at Day Break

Life is a matter of conjugation
(Hey diddly daddy)
I am alive, you are alive
(Hickory dickory dock)
He is dead, they are dead
(The man ran up the clock)
Conjugal, jug, con-man, coitus
Craftsman, crafty, cop
(Little Bo Peep come blow your horn.)
Woman children man
For little Jack Horner
Is in his corner
Eating
(Hey, nonny nonny)
And we all run down.

(This must have been written on the farm, probably in the mid-80's, because it's the only time I got up at daybreak (to milk my two goats) before I drove fifty-five miles to my academic job at Cottey College in Nevada, Missouri.)

Eleven Percent

I read recently
(I think it might have been from the Mayo Clinic),
That optimists live eleven to fourteen percent
Longer than those
Who aren't so hopeful.
Interesting.
I wonder if these people
Just re-interpret what is going on
To craft a new reality
From the clay of what's before them.
As you can tell:
I don't call myself an optimist.
So do I start thinking about what comes
After the next four years are over
When someone else is leading the country,
So that I can live longer?
I probably need to dig around
And find some optimists to see how they are doing
Right now.
(However, I'm going to have to exclude
The MAGAs,
Because they wouldn't be a good model
For living
For someone like me,
Because I treasure facts,
Not hats.)
I'm just not sure where to look
For these other people.
Now that I think of it
I can't imagine my mother

Having changed her outlook
To a rosier one either
From her German-American stoicism
And frugality,
Washing plastic bags
And recycling just about everything
Before there was a word for it.
Based upon what I read, she would have lived to be 104-107.
I guess 94 was a good enough age,
Without being an optimist.
I feel a lot better now that I think of that.

The '55 Chevy

My mother's '55 Chevy was a classy green and white model
That she kept clean and polished
And always parked in the garage to keep it that way,
For years and years.

It was a car that required muscles to drive
Just turning the wheel
Or opening and closing the windows
Or even applying the brakes.
Nothing was automatic.

It kept on running
Purring like a kitten,
Until it turned into an old cat,
And then this thing and then that
Required my brothers to figure out how to fix it.
They were good that way
Until they thought my Mom couldn't or shouldn't drive anymore.
So they disconnected the battery
To make her think it was time to give it a rest.

Now I'm the '55 Chevy.
I used to be polished with long shining hair;
Now it's not so shiny.
Now there's always something that needs fixing.
If it's not my brakes or back or spark plugs or heart,
It's something only the computer or MRI can assess
And often doesn't.
To make matters worse, my brothers are no longer around
To cheer me up or cheer me on.

But like my mother's Chevy
That later went to another driver and then a younger one
For many more years,
I know this old frame
Will honk its way into the next garage,
For safekeeping.

What'll You Do?

When the well is going dry,
When the sky is blue
And you just wanted rain?
When your best friend
Is showing signs of something,
That sure looks dire.
And you can't even tell her.

What'll you do
When all you want to do
Is walk in the woods,
Or on the beach,
But your body doesn't want
To move
That much
For that long.

It's not easy
When time is marching on,
And people are dying
Who should be answering the phone
As they always did,
When you needed them.
Now they are gone
And who even knows where?
Because there seem to be no answers
For any of the questions we have,
Other than what to eat
For dinner.
And who will cook it.

At Last?

We're having the last Black Krim tonight—
My favorite plant this year.
This tomato first grown in Crimea, who knows when,
But long ago.
Appropriate, it seems, to support Ukraine,
Symbolically
With our stomachs
As well as our arms.
We will miss our Black Krim,
And grow it again next year
When Ukraine will be free again, we hope
Of the blight of Russia's war.

We mourn the loss of other things and other people,
Those in the Middle East
Who have lost their homes and hospitals and schools,
And lives,
And their hope for the future.
For me, I mourn the loss of my family,
Who can no longer invite me into their homes.
The last close one gone now
To a different kind of home.

And will this be the last election
Before my own end?
Or the end of something more important:
The ability to watch the news
Without weeping
For the old days
Of normal give and take?

Without guns in bedside tables
Of those who want to turn the tables
On everyone else?

My mother-in-law used to say
To her growing boys:
"You just make me tired."
I think she was right—
There are a lot of growing boys
Out there
And I can't wait for them to grow up
At last,
Because it's making me tired
Too.

Poem from My Younger Self

There's no running and hiding anymore;
It's time to settle down and forget all those
 "Now I'm going to do nexts."
Just look in the mirror:
You are starting to look like your mother, girl.
Sure, at your age, she still got permanents
Every few months,
And your hair is straight the way you fixed it when you were thirty,
But you have her varicose veins,
and high blood pressure,
and your back hurts,
Oh, and you had the same hysterectomy,
For goodness sake.
Give it all a rest.
Time to dance around the May Pole,
Let it all hang out,
And then just take a nap.

(Written January 18, 2024: The day I turned in my heart monitor, got a crown for my tooth, and remembered the death of my second husband, twenty-eight years earlier.)

ACKNOWLEDGEMENTS

I am extremely grateful to my friends, Marcia Conrad, Joan Inzinga, Nancy Mitchell, Elsie Nespor, Beth Parker, Dianne Wilichowski, and my cousin Maxine Gehrt, who have provided continuous support and encouragement for my bringing this little book of poems to completion. They have listened willingly and even with enthusiasm to the vintage poems I've resurrected from the past and to each new poem as I've dragged it off the computer. I would also like to acknowledge the support and advice that Vana Nespor has given me for bringing this document to press. I can't thank her enough for making it all seem easy. Well, to her.

Finally, I would like to acknowledge the role that Louisa Loveridge-Gallas (my sunbathing friend from the 60's) has played in inspiring me with her love of crafting poetry and the work that she has shared with me and her other ardent readers of her publications over the many years of our friendship.